THE LIGHTHOUSE BECKONS

Poems By

Juanita J. Martin

To Marilyn,
Thank you for your support.

Love,
Juanita J. Martin

The Lighthouse Beckons
ISBN: 978-0-9742604-8-8

Library of Congress Control Number: 2012914231

First printing

Cover art: View of the Cape Florida lighthouse,
Bill Baggs State Park, Key Biscayne, Miami Florida
Photo by Rudy Umans, Photographer

Printed in the United States by Morris Publishing®
3212 East Highway 30
Kearney, NE 68847
1-800-650-7888

Grateful acknowledgement to Al Young,
California Poet Laureate (2005-2008),
for his words of praise.

Grateful acknowledgement to Redwood Writers
for professional relationships and friendships
throughout the years.

Table of Contents

Poems 1-100

Table of Contents (cont'd)

Table of Contents (cont'd)

Table of Contents (cont'd)

Table of Contents (cont'd)

Other writing credits/ related credits

Notes

I thank God for giving me the gift of creativity to share with the world.

Introduction

The Lighthouse Beckons is a book
of broad-based, incisive, sometimes ethereal
poems. *The Lighthouse Beckons* invites you
to sample its various forms of light:
the light that is apparent,
the contrast of light and dark,
or the luminescence of one's soul.
I chose the title *The Lighthouse Beckons,*
because poetry is like a beacon that lights the way.
Through the words I have written, I have become
that lighthouse, sharing my light with those
who have a kinship with poetic value.
I hope these poems will enlighten the reader
and become a sanctuary. I invite the reader
to read each poem, receive its light,
and become a beacon for the rest of the world.
—**Juanita J. Martin**, Fairfield's 1st Poet Laureate 2010-2012

THE LIGHTHOUSE BECKONS

OWNERS OF THE LIGHT

Bridges of light that do not flicker,
luminous pathways guide souls to a river,
where they stand at the mouth.
The dead hold hands in celebration.
Families gather to remember—
they present songs and verses,
honor memories, burn their wishes.
As colors dance in the smoke,
they embrace the inner glow, share in the gift.
Spirits rise from the embers to rest on cloud-pillows
where love is a portal through which they enter;
our thoughts weighted from that day.

DISCOVERING CALIFORNIA'S NATURE

A dimly-lit sky is trimmed in shades of lavender and blue.
Along a California highway, a poppy dances a slow waltz.
I stop to take a deep breath, taste the richness of life.

The long arm of nature embraces me
as a mother holds her child.
The sigh of a summer wind is her lullaby.
The sun's glowing essence satisfies;
it illuminates my innocence.

The soothing blanket of water engulfs me like a womb.
For a brief moment I return to that world
to examine nature from inside
through the comfort of my mother's eyes.

Although I walk among the redwoods
as they peek into God's window,
this westerner's shore is still a mystery
where I am just a suckling at her breast.
Struggling to find my way, I latch on
and drink until I am full.

BATS IN THE CORRIDOR

A storage locker becomes unbearable,
as squeaky wheels roll across cement floors.
As I enter the hallway, escaping eyes loom.

Cowering in a corner, dodging a bat's wing,
calling out to cold walls and no one replies,
reminds me of the past.
Once again I am alone, afraid,
with just the sincerity of my heart.

After disappearing into shadows,
a bat soars through an open window;
a jolt to signify I am starting over.

Remembering yesterday,
I am distanced from today
and the corridor of my mind.

RETREAT

An obscure road asks me to travel her again,
so I close my eyes to the city.
The country's falsetto voice calls me back.
The deafening sounds of the daily drone
become a windy chorus of the trees.

I am like a child that loves to play.
I can retrace the reticent feel
of nature's breath on my skin
as I stray under nonchalant skies
like the first time, every time.

Within my own backyard
lies a serene path of rejuvenation;
suddenly, I am sinking into the velvet grass.

TRINKETS OF LOVE

I am the tarnished ring you once wore,
a symbol of love long forgotten,
cast aside in a box,
unable to shine.

Just another lackluster memory
that scars and stains:
an old house, an old car, an old woman—
once new, once able to seduce,
now discarded with your youth.

You stare out a window
of an old house at an old car,
remembering an old woman.

She lies next to me, unframed,
scarred by you,
stained with a diamond—
just another trinket.

INVISIBLE

I make my entrance at the end.
Perhaps that's why you do not see me.
Taken for granted, a closer of the show,
whisking through the aisles,
after the wine, cuisine,
after the others take their bow.

A phantom shuffling used dinnerware,
where epicurean delights once were,
with no tip, thank-you, or gracious hello.
I disappear into the back wall,
between the water pitchers and ice machine.

This is where the clean and the dirty are friendly,
where the chefs know my name,
where I appear as myself.

TWIST IN THE HEAT

Scorching summer sky, raging wind
consuming like wildfire,
sifting domiciles, forgotten treasures
throughout the countryside.
Spiral cloud churning, claiming souls,
life's discards, as we melt into our skin,
holding onto the intangible.

NIGHT WATCH

The night pulls back its layers, exposing its true self.
The moon's light shines on a badge,
as a uniformed silhouette appears.
Instincts and coffee are his only companions
in this wintry deluge.

A lone drifter turns a corner into emptiness.
A solitary shack stands between him and the chill;
it moves through the air like a pendulous death.
An uneasy feeling stirs within his mind.
He reaches into a soulless dark, shivering,
wanting reassurance, restoration for that which is lost.
Some call it serenity, some call it destiny.
Others call it shelter from the coldness of life.

Face to face, they seek the will of their spirits.
The homeless man looks for comfort
in the eyes of the officer.
The guard looks for courage to examine
the warmth of a stranger's smile.

OPEN HEART, OPEN ROAD

Heart wide open,
no pit stops,
just cruise control
along life's highway.
A drop-top Chevy,
an adventurous trek
on the way to love,
between hope and happiness,
road wide open;
my soul reflects the wear.

FASCINATION OF A WISHING WELL

What is the fascination of a wishing well?
With high hopes, a coin is released, so is a wish,
into the mesmerizing deep, a swell of living water,
reflections of youthful pride.

We cleave to the promise
of its magical power.
We are under its spell,
seduced to believe in our dreams.

What is the fascination of a wishing well?
Some decades later, a dilapidated form
surrounded by weeds and rusty metal,
pulls us back into its depths.

It belonged in a time when water ran free,
when we ran free,
from the boundaries of our souls,
into the miracle that lies in our hands.

THE WICK

An old lantern burned through the hourglass of time.
It once shone in the Old West, lighting a litany
of darkened lives—the rise and fall of railroad depots,
the last dance of a harlot's petticoat,
the making of a gunslinger's reign.

An old woman sat reading by a lantern.
The lantern did not flicker
as kerosene soaked its wick.
She watched the light sway its hypnotic glow.
It was like a beacon, guiding her soul.

The old woman closed the book
and the final chapter of her life.
Just as she had lived,
her light still shone
like the ancient lantern.

The lantern becomes a haunting symbol of light.
We are like the wick.
It reminds us that between birth and death,
it's not the life of the wick that matters,
it's the burning.

THE WIND

The illusion of the wind leaves one awestruck:
its sweet caress of nature's bounty,
the sunlit brush of its invisible hand,
the cool whisper through trees,
and gentle strokes of oceanic calm.

In its curious flight,
the wind mocks the earth
by unleashing its wrath,
then descends upon the dust
as a musical whirl, to dance a nightly dream.

The wind is an enigma
that reveals mankind's daily discards.
It's a familiar sound in the dark,
an escort down secret pathways;
it's a spirit, mesmerizing light.

SOUL ON FIRE

Seated on the couch, examining the brilliant
effigy of a childhood memory,
entranced by the crackling of the fire
and the sway of auburn-colored flames.

They warm the cold place in my heart,
singe the roughness of my soul,
remove the harshness of my mind.

Now I am deeply content,
tempered with an internal glow.
Staring into the fire's abyss
is similar to life: it's raw on entry,
a slow burn, yet purifying in the end.

BLESSING OF THE TREES

Arrival of a new day;
I stand in awe.
Hues of blue and purple sky
open like an umbrella.
The trees salute in full dress;
colors of spring surround me.
I am baptized with the spray
of a recent rainfall.
The fresh breath of the season,
sweet pungent air
inoculates my nose,
releasing its power.
Something tapped my shoulder;
I felt the dance of the wind.
I fell down and prayed,
thanking God for the trees.

WARD OF ANGELS

They arrived as soldiers armed with compassion.
Carrying the elixir of the gods, they roamed.
Whispers of content, gentle stirs
of those ravaged with disease,
brought delight to these caring souls.
When their duty was done,
they disappeared into a blissful horizon.

With charts in hand, today's young Nightingales
walk with the anticipation of an unborn son,
fulfilling deeds left behind.
Those that came before, now salute.
The race for them has ended
as they pass on batons of hope.
Their spirits smile from beyond the walls
as they dance ceremoniously, awaiting their wings.

WAITING ROOM

They sit in comfortable chairs,
heads bowed as if to pray.
They move to the edge of their seats
when the phone rings.
With a pocketful of hope,
they cling to the sounds of their own heartbeats.

They contemplate their own mortality
as voices beckon from inside.
The taste of a forgotten meal still lingers on their lips.
Drool dries on their chest
as snores drown the world outside.

A clock is an enemy that erases their light.
Loneliness and fear surround
a room full of strangers.
Decorated walls seem more like a prison
and God holds the only key.

Souls are spared in the early dawn,
as the sun comes over the hill.
Nighttime is now a figment
and the waiting room is content in silence.

COAT HANGER TALES

Mysteries, snippets of the dead
and the living remain in a closet.
Part of us is attached to the outer garment,
the one we wear and the one we disguise.

Hangers are exposed to convenient indiscretions,
aftermaths of societal rages,
humiliation of youthful taunts.
Symbols of souls are briefly
examined in this symbiotic state.

What tales would they tell?

Through them, we could unravel our past,
solve puzzles of life.
Would we dismiss their honesty?
Could we shun their infinite wisdom?
Do we fear they would put us on display?
Perhaps they would reveal too much of our secret self.

Destined to be our instruments
to place the world upon,
hangers exist inside the darkness,
while we pretend in the light.

WOUNDED

An abandoned bird nurses a fractured wing.
A troubled youth seeks comfort from a stranger.
A child grows up in a broken home.
Vaults of confusion, years of torment,
disguised by masks of love are razors to their soul.

Desperate attempts are made to be heard,
to be rescued. They retreat to dark, empty nests
to bandage their hearts.
Scars are left as twisted martyrs continue to bleed.

Now in the light,
souls are released unharmed.
The world is full again
of beautiful creatures
soaring with unclipped wings.

NEVER SAID GOODBYE

Calm spring air carried stings of pain,
as two lives wrestled in peril on separate shores.
A glance at a vase, a stir from an empty hallway,
brought a poignant sigh from a daughter's lips,
as she prepared for the news of her mother.

Somber clouds hovered like a weight on a daughter's soul.
Eyes were heavy, a mind too full.
A sense of relief came, doubts lingered,
as her heart rushed to her mother's bedside.
She wished she could have said goodbye.

Instead, she swirled in the darkness,
to a lonely dance without music.
She relived untold stories of a broken existence,
with no peace, no joyful exchange
between herself and her mother.
She longed for the voice of love never heard,
tender kisses never felt.
Forgiveness was a bitter pill upon her tongue,
as she released her mother, the past,
into an empty California skyline.

The sun ushered in just beyond the hills
to warm the coldness above and below.
As dew lifted from the trees,
silence fell like a snowflake
in the softness of that April day.

SOMEWHERE IN THE NIGHT

A black-robed creature appeared
in one man's nightmares.
This man found himself high on a beam,
searching for a final answer.
Fixed with visions of a
lonely skyline and dark water,
he bids farewell to the city.

Somewhere in the night,
just as the fog lifts, another drifter,
a nameless figure, appears troubled.
A shadow of a man, unnoticed,
sinks into the depths,
a true elixir for all his pain.

Somewhere in the night,
a stranger arrives on that same forbidden path,
bewildered, contemplating his own end.
Voices from the deep warn him away,
shouting their mistakes,
hoping that a soul would be spared.

Somewhere in the night, for once,
death gave back life;
on this night, ghosts do not wail
at the wall of remembrance.

WIND CHIME SERENADE

Hear the melody of the chimes
as they dance in the whistling wind:
soft as the flutter of a bird's wing,
the clamor of a thousand bells,
an orchestra of the sky.

The purity of the sound is esoteric;
not influenced by mankind,
revealing as an alabaster moon
in the shadow of winter.

I lie undisturbed
by the rhythm of the night:
the ebb and flow of the tide,
nature's unrelenting flourish
under the God-music to my soul.

WHITE DIAMONDS

Crystalline forms, nature's jewels surround us
like an etched frame of life inside a window.
An explosion of white lands upon the ground
sifting and molding the landscape,
dusting treetops and passersby.

The brilliance captures our youth,
its essence dances in our dreams;
its charm disrobes our inhibitions.
We are caught in its mystery:
white diamonds in the sand,
white diamonds from the sky.

VOICES

From out of the nocturnal journey
of our past are voices of creativity—
some audible, some silent.

We give praise to the masters
who wove the tapestry we now bask in.
They opened tombs of our minds,
abysmal corners of our lives.

We can live out written
and unwritten dreams
from one generation to the next.

How great is it that hearts that beat,
long after their death, guide the future,
while finding their way to other souls!

WINTER ESCAPE

The trees appear like apparitions
waving their ghostly arms,
while little ones scream and play,
until daylight disappears.
Icy daggers hang from the eaves,
as homes sag under winter's weight.

Watching a cozy evening fire
takes me back to our untarnished youth.
Hot, frothy drinks cured early morning shivers.
We made angels in the snow,
wrote silly messages on frosted panes.

Now in the winter of our lives, we escape,
ignoring blusterous winds,
the scraping of our bones,
to rediscover the magic
and innocence of snowflakes.

SPRING ENLIGHTENMENT

Dew plants kisses upon the green
as a countryside awakens.
Her beauty is whitewater cascading.

Birds unveil the dawn
as rain falls in soft concerto
upon waxy thin blades.

Airy petals sprinkle their essence
along the ground
as sun-stained leaves cling from above.

Mother Nature's palette
is mixed to perfection.
Creatures gather to witness a rebirth.

Tepid winds conjure an array,
casting scented spells
that charge the senses.

Horizons beckon with soothing clouds
to bless the nectar of the gods.
Yesterday sheds its garment with pride.

Mankind ponders to drink the living bounty,
carve pieces of the moon and the stars;
all are portraits painted on the canvas of my eyes.

POINT REYES GHOST

Over shorebirds, she rolls in.
She spreads herself like a see-through blanket,
over the landscape.
Her mysterious form frames the peninsula
like a still photograph.

Her thin drape unveils distant towns,
creatures rising in the early dawn.
Sunlight makes cameo appearances
through her haunting mass.

She moves stealthily, blocking the lighthouse.
It stands proud like a saintly tower,
lifting its finger of judgment toward a crowded shore.

Unaware of her presence, strangers swarm
for a last glance at the mighty gray whale,
as a mist quietly slips into Tomales Bay.

The cool, damp, January air invigorates,
yet chills the souls of the watchers,
as if they had just witnessed an apparition.

UNDERNEATH A PLAYFUL MOON

Seductive breezes stroke our locks,
in the warm summer air.
Gentle rain falls slowly on the ground,
on the delicacy of our souls.

As we frolic, long stalks, soft petals
press and glide against our skin.
The moon captures our shadows
in its countenance,
leaving our minds to wander
as we echo the howls of the night.

Water glistens, the sap oozes,
while trees overlook
the mold of our torsos.
Gazing up at the sky, we suddenly realize
we are merely backdrops
for the sensual scene of Mother Earth.

MOONBEAMS

I have always imagined that the moonbeams
bouncing about a celestial plane,
were God's footprints in the nocturnal sky.

They would pave the way,
flickering like a giant candle burning,
as he moved among the stars.

The softness of the light emanated
like gentle eyes watching over the earth.
Nights resembled days under the luminescence.

At certain times the rays accelerated,
like jets flying across the world.
Perhaps this was when God was dancing.

A QUIET FIREPLACE

Guilt rippled amid snores of an out-stretched torso
as he shared piles of memories with the sofa.
A half-eaten meal graced the dining room table
beside an empty bottle of wine and a broken glass.
Echoes of bedroom fantasies replayed
as collective sighs of passion
were accentuated by a drunken stupor.
A romantic interlude faded into a cool dewdrop morn,
while flickers of burning embers remained.

VORTEX

The valley's wind is like a vortex.
Our souls are caught in its whirl,
as it tosses yesterday aside.
The rest of nature bows to it.
Today we stand against it,
search through its aftermath,
gather pieces of our lives
to find strength
and meaning for tomorrow.

OUT OF THE DARKNESS

He walks the night, mind shattered,
wearing badges of affliction.
Shards of sadness remain;
his soul bleeding,
he succumbs to the weight of darkness.
That mistress of fate beckons him to sleep,
to escape his prison, the cruelty of existence.
The ache of regret came like an angel
to quicken a dying breath,
in time to lead him toward daylight.

LIFE TURNS

Life is a choir;
its praises you sing.
Life is a schoolbook,
preparing you for its tests.
Life is a dog;
it has you chasing its tail and licking its wounds.
Life is like the moon;
it shines upon you, lighting dark pathways,
then hides its face like a coward.
Life is a pyramid;
its mysterious eye watches you
while you travel corner to corner,
only to find that you never left.
Life is a table;
you dine upon it openly and intimately,
until you are full.
Life puts on its signal to take a turn.
You find joy, at times, but your heart does not beat.
Life takes another turn.
You yield temporarily, cautiously,
but keep going forward.

NAVIGATION OF THE SUN

The sun navigates its brilliant shine beyond the trees
to orchestrate tomorrow's existence,
light the way of the barn swallow back to its nest,
illuminate the soul of the earth,
power nature's heartbeat.
A civilization in need of warmth
awakens to her smile.

THE HUMMINGBIRD'S SONG

As the frost lifts, a hummingbird awakens from his sleep.
He is sitting pretty in ruby-red
like a king on a throne.
He stands out from the rest of nature,
humming as he takes off.

He lands on a fir tree chirping away,
with the world at his feet.
He swoops down for a taste of nectar
from some nearby flowers.
The hummingbird lifts his tiny wings
to continue the journey,
as the sun sneaks through the clouds.

I love to listen to his song
that plays softly in my ears.
It is sweet to my soul;
the beginning of many hopeful mornings.

TRANQUILITY

Capture the moon's light over the ocean,
witness the enchanting beauty of the stars,
feel the wind's calming embrace,
seek the gentleness of the clouds,
as nature becomes a deep, somnolent rapture.

SOUL DANCE

Hard times, uncertainties abound
as society vies for sustenance.
Where do we all fit in?
Are we resigned to the privileged versus the poor?

A soul in need asks another soul in need,
"Can I have some money for food?"
A desperate plea led to a sinking heart,
in the presence of shame.

I questioned my feelings, but declined in fear.
My vulnerability, his integrity: who will win?
Eventually, my soul danced to the other side.

He disappeared in the dust of my contemplation.
Trying to avoid his soul, I found my own.

VALENTINE'S DAY: LOST IN THE MEANING

Valentine's Day, a celebration of professed love,
full of symbols, hearts, flowers, treats—
couples give in honor of the lover's holiday.

What if the holiday no longer has meaning?
What if the love is really gone?
What if it never existed?
Do we still go through the motions of relationships?

Two lovers play each other's heartstrings,
hope for a better tune.
They give flowers, a pretty substitute
for saying "I love you."

Chocolate or other confections taste good
but won't replace the kiss that was sweeter.
A card—a voiceless messenger—
doesn't speak a true sentiment.

Lost in the meaning with no words to love by,
lovers vie for each other's hearts
by performing ritualistic exchanges,
while trying to ease their own souls once more.

FLICKER

I was filled with determination
An imaginative flair
That framed my tough exterior
I burned with illumination
Bright enough so others would know
I was only reflecting what consumed my soul
I was ready to set the world on fire
With what I had inside
But I was just another flicker
In a sea of flames

WHETTING MY APPETITE

Life is a meal I consume
one course at a time,
light, airy, and refreshing
like a crisp salad
with splashes of color
selectively sprinkled,
tasteful and juicy
like a succulent foul
seasoned to perfection.

Nothing heavy
to mask the blandness
of my soul.
Nothing strong to drown regret
or overstate elation.

Something that fills the void
in between dreams,
something sweet, smooth,
that titillates the senses.
Something warm, comfortable,
like my morning brew
that boldly awakens me
on a new journey.

BURIED

Beneath the haunted woman is the child,
Undermined by foes in familiar guises. She sat quietly,
Reminiscing the pain in shadows, torments,
Inscribed on her soul like a headstone.
Even though her heart survived, the fond memories are
Dead, a silent reflection of the childhood she did not have.

BUTTERFLY DREAMS

In my dreams, I am a butterfly
spreading my freedom wings,
perched above the world,
above the madness,
on the flower of my destiny;
bold with shimmering colors
that playfully romp in the sun
like those psychedelic days of
tie-dyed shirts and ripped jeans,
when I dared to slay the dragon
of hate in front of me,
when I cared enough to frolic
in sun-stroked meadows,
taste the fruit of my youth,
don the courage to preach wisdom
and curse hypocrisy
with a smile on my face.

LANDSCAPE OF WINTER

No wonderland to call our own
like those in fairytales
that sprinkle dust upon a throne
to bestow a magic kingdom.

Treetops bow as they wake
to nature's painted chill,
which brings sudden death for the sake
of a winter's fated wrath.

Creatures hide in secret places,
while embers crack and sputter
to soothe the sting upon our faces
as we leave to hibernate.

Rooftops belt a single sigh
to release the drifts that fall,
as snowplows rush a darkened sky
to tame the great white beast.

TEMPEST DAWN

Lightening flew like fireworks,
as thunder shook the windows violently.
Nature's attack was enough to raise the dead,
but I did not hear the alarm's shrill sound.

Morning revealed neighbors competing for the freeway,
disguising their rage by peeling on asphalt.
They rushed off to unfulfilling jobs and ill-mannered bosses.
It seemed like the whole world was on edge.

As I showered, water seared my bottom like a hot iron.
The pot boiled with strong coffee that singed my lips.
The toaster burned my last piece of bread;
I woofed down charred remains, as I headed for the door.

Then the car refused to start, after several attempts.
It was as if all the machines were angry, somewhat rebellious.
Perhaps they also had enough, wanted a rest,
from performing their duties once more.

I was just a cog in the wheel;
a committed fool
with her nose to the grind,
another member of the rat race.

Now I am quietly sitting at my desk,
applying makeup with deliberate strokes,
ignoring the phone and the computer screen,
blind to the prison of partitions that surround me.

LIGHT IN THE FOREST

One light in the forest
Man plays in nature's retreat
Careless crimson and yellow
Help rid the foliage
Silence the beast
Mankind masks the guilt
With a casual plea
No justice for the lowly order
Whose souls still bleed

HIGH SCHOOL MADNESS

Those foul whispers
fall from my mind,
a convergence of pain
wells in my eyes.

Awkward teenage years,
contrived affectations come to the forefront.
I stand in a sea of ugliness, sadness,
where the pretty judge the latest trend.

Swept away in tides of doubt and desire,
agonizing whether I was good enough
to be the dream date of virile young men,
to feel the spotlight on my face.

I cower from the bus to the classroom chair
to disappear behind a mound of books.
The teacher's voice fades behind
homeroom gossip and bathroom smoke clouds.

Through the haze of the hallway,
contemptuous eyes follow me
from the basketball court to the softball field,
where I bury sins and my naiveté.

SIERRA SUN

Sierra sun, that luminous blaze
that drapes over pock-marked mountains,
bakes the clouds intensely.

Her bursting orange glow
shifts the earth's mood,
lights a subdued sky.

She exposes folds upon the landscape
with traces of sienna, forest green, blended.
Her flames sear the mountain's basin east to west.

The fiery dome consumes as the days wear long,
becoming an iron burning an imprint
upon our souls.

LEFTOVERS

A romance is rekindled.
A place in the heart is prepared for him: the one.
He's worth the battle, worth the pain.
In the end, love withstands.

A casserole is reheated.
A place is prepared for one at a table for two.
Tears are dabbed with a napkin.
Reminiscing brings smiles momentarily.

An appetite fulfilled, a void left over.
Leftover meals stain the tongue,
leftover scars stain the soul;
they both leave the same taste: bittersweet.

PAPER PUSHER

Behind a wall of mounting trees,
a veteran of the pool sits tapping
the latest throng of memos.
The strain of carpal tunnel
does not inhibit those willing digits.
The paper traffic does not cease—
just like the dreams of many,
they are delayed
in a side basket of tomorrows.

MAGNET

Melodic voice, seductive smile,
An attractive missile of sexuality
Guided toward vulnerability where
Notions of love prick receptive souls.
Eventually compliant hearts will succumb;
Thrills await them if they dare.

JEALOUSY

Juvenile intention rise,
Expressed by wicked souls.
A beast within them rages,
Leaps in desperation;
One will to survive.
Unleashing their scourge across the plains,
Societal lions prey at a price—
Yes, even death.

ART EMBRACES THE PAST ©2005

Eyes of long ago
relate desperate tales of industrial reign
in a grand house of history.
Through magic of an artist's medium,
artifacts take another breath of life
in the New Millennial Age.
Myriads of concepts blend
to accentuate a simpler style and place
that's impervious to the span of time.

THE COLLECTOR

A grubby hand reaches down,
swoops a can out of the trash and adds it to a sack.
A man of modest means appears from the alley.
His face is pale and drawn,
his lips are parched and shriveled.
Covered in an overcoat, he begins his day at 6 am,
along with a beat cop on the corner.

His weathered eyes roam, as he hobbles along,
amid routine deliveries, inner city hierarchies,
and hustles of the streets.
Some people think they know his story;
he's a man most would ignore.

He leads a life of simplicity,
not bound by conformity;
he lives honestly.
He's not stealing or begging bread;
he can face the man in the mirror.

No one can fathom why he lives this way.
Perhaps he had it all once—treasures included,
but discarded it all like trash.
Now the trash is his lifeline.
Each day he redeems the cans he redeems himself.

WHEN LOVE DROWNS

Alone in a cold tide,
I reach the surface momentarily,
only to be pulled back under.

The monotony swells.
Survival is a struggle
as time ticks away.

Heart's beating sporadically,
in the murky aftermath
of love gone wrong.

It's a casualty of relationships
where two people ride the waves
on a junket called passion.

Romance is a castaway in the dark
with no rescue for the lonely,
whose shore of hope is just a mirage.

Waiting to be rescued,
a hush surrounds me;
I'm in the deep, drowning.

OASIS

Mother Earth can no longer feed her children.
She is dying of poison, concoctions of man.
She is laced with burnt skies and polluted shores.
Now, with too many sunrises,
her soul bakes, her heart bleeds.

She trudges onward, in spite of her afflictions,
knowing tomorrow is still a promise to be fulfilled.
Yet today, I can still bow in her moonlight
to escape life's vapid drain,
to discover yet another realm of my oasis.

PLEASURE

Turning on the light
The knob round in our hand
The luminescence becomes our clay
We mold ourselves in its radiance

VAN GOGH's SUMMER

Sunflowers, drunken with wind
Are suspended along a fence,
Near a rustic bungalow
Mists of water from a pond
Too faint for their thirst
Hues of blue, burning sky
Fill an open window
Luminous rays escape
Embracing innocence
Golden petals fall
Consumed by hot earth
Immortalized before me
Like those on the wall
Quickened by the palette of van Gogh

THE LANGUAGE OF HER EYES

She gazed into his lonely heart.
Enchanting melodies played upon her soul,
bodies trembled in sweet revelations.
Voices framed in silence,
tender moments captured,
images of romantic interludes were exchanged
through the language of her eyes.

FLASHES

No folded or torn edges of photographs
No dusty heirlooms filed away
Life's precious moments are held electronically
Frame by living color frame
Images captured up close
A time capsule of treasures
We can turn on and turn off
Just like those visions of life
In our head,
Perfect or not
We accept them as memories
That won't fade away
Memories we can recall
With a touch a button

BLIZZARD OF 1983

Power lines sagged and swayed under winter's steady assault.
The streets were as empty as a hobo's pockets.
Cars that were left behind became an auto graveyard.
It was as if the whole city went into hiding.
Wrapped like a cocoon, I pushed against freezing temps,
a blinding snowfall, just to get to work.
Buses and jitneys were scarce at the time.
The thought of waiting kept me moving,
as cold air trapped my breath.
I felt the sky closing in under the flutter of my heart.

The wind wailed upon me, as I stumbled down city blocks
that seemed to go on forever.
Visibility escaped along with the presence of daylight.
I was like a soldier in battle, trudging through
a jungle of white powder.
The snow hit the ground like bombs all around me.
At times, I took cover under overhangs of buildings.
As the bleakness continued, it felt like my body
was on the receiving end of nature's apocalypse.

A RIVER RUNS THROUGH ME

Walking along the American River bed,
I lick the crisp mountain air. It glides
across my tongue like summer raindrops in a forest.
My soul tingles, as I disappear into
the ecstasy of a wet dreamscape.

The rushing waves are ephemeral
as I bathe my spirit.
So effortless, weightless, I move—life into life.
A cacophony is created by the smashing
of blackened rocks,
that leave an angled wear pattern.

A symphony bounces off the water
with the boldness of Bach and Tchaikovsky,
the force of Beethoven and Verdi,
or the calm of Mozart and Vivaldi.

The wind beckons through the trees,
softly, gently, like a mysterious hand
directing a path, my heart,
as a river runs through me.

ON SOLID GROUND

Words from my soul
Roam as whispered gems
To the ears of mankind
They entreat
Inform
Enlighten
Shield against entropy
To become imprints on solid ground

HESITANT FLOWER

I was that hesitant flower
That failed to bloom in the spring
Failed to dine on the sun's invitation
Failed to drink the water of life
Failed to grow in the presence of earth
Failed to overcome the spoils of nature
Left to stand against the prevailing wind.

TRANSLUCENT SKY

Underneath
Waiting for the clouds
To cry
Void of darkness
No shadow to swallow the light
My soul reached out
To grab the sun
Which danced about
In a translucent sky

AT THE RESTAURANT

At the restaurant, I sit alone pondering,
while some patrons distract themselves
with scandal sheets.
Others search for healing for an ailing economy.

Conversation pours hotter than the coffee—
secrets are revealed in a friendly one on one,
diversions from co-workers are shared
and housewives exchange vicarious woes.

As thoughts weigh heavy on my mind,
I take notice of people around me.
Amidst society's problems, the aromas,
the flavors, and a strong brew,
I am still trapped by idle chit-chat.

LONGING FOR THE SUN

It had been a cold and grinding winter
that devoured parts of spring.
The sun didn't greet me each morning.
Sometimes it was not seen for days,
as dark clouds hovered into the night.

I longed to absorb the sun's rays,
bask in its radiance.
I welcomed its warm exuberant arms
that embraced me like a lover,
from the first hello to the last goodbye.

Summer came in hard and fast.
It made no apologies for its entrance.
The saturation of a summer sun
cradled the universe with blueness of skies
and crystal-clear waters.

I was a boat drifting in the foggy shadows
of past disappointments.

The sun was the gust of wind my lifeless sails needed.
It reminded me of life, a new life with brighter days.

WITHERING OF TREES

I awakened to that silent doom of getting old.
My eyelids struggled to open,
as I wrestled with the blanket.

I turned on the lamp for my morning routine.
Life appeared before me in shades of black and white.
I yawned and stretched,
as I fumbled my way to the bathroom.

I gazed at some old trees, just outside my window.
Lines of deterioration were apparent;
limbs were brittle and sagging.
The bark was peeling and rotting on the grass.

I examined my face, looking for signs of aging—
dry, pitted skin, spots or wrinkles that came through.
I was in a race against time,
trying to grab pieces of yesterday.

The trees were strong once too, pushing against nature,
against the world, in order to take their rightful place.
They were not concerned with the past
or the face in the mirror.

UNBRIDLED

We met anonymously. Two stalled beings on the same quest.
You pressed your silken tameness against a brazen soul.
We cuddled in the whispery afterglow of a shy moon.

Our hearts danced to a nuance.
Heads held high, we sighed in relief
from corrals of familiarity and stale yesterdays,
when the wind failed to blow.

Minds adrift,
the minutes, the hours moved
like a jagged-edged blade slicing away.
Throughout the night we romped amorously.
Our bodies were delivered along the shore,
as water pounded the rocks in ecstasy.

Two kindred spirits escaped their reins
for a run of guilt-free passion, love optional.

DAYDREAMS

What are daydreams?
They are desires,
fantasies in radiant fashion,
attachments to the subconscious,
that won't let go.

Our thoughts are played out
on a stage of actors we direct.
We revel in our own production.

Daydreams make life interesting—
they allow our minds to wander,
paint the town in vivid pastels,
while we drift along without a care in the world.

FIREFLIES

As a child, I used to play with fireflies
in the warm, New Jersey air.
I was fascinated by their burning, yellow glow.

They flickered on and off,
like a luminescent bulb.
I felt the freedom from their wings.

At times, I treated them as pets.
They flit onto my finger,
like a bird on a perch.

We had our ritual dance
underneath the stars,
but they were not to be owned.

I released them back
to the night sky,
where I became the lowly order.

THE PEACE OF NIGHT

Sometimes the night can be a friend.
The calm, gentle, almost serendipitous cover
releases the strain of daytime,
quiets the noise in our head.

The nighttime hold us still in one place,
to examine the universe we take for granted—
the fixed solemnness of the sky with nature's radiant light,
the vanilla softness of the stars, an incandescent moon.

Occasional sighs of earth, the heartbeat of man,
compete for comfort in the nocturnal surrender.
We lie under its shadow;
we caress the darkness with our souls.
We are children nestled in its arms
with nothing but its whispers,
and the sound of the whippoorwill against our breath.

DREAMSCAPES

My mind is adrift,
as I lie in a bed of calla lilies.
The warmth of the sun looms overhead,
the serenity of a brook trickles nearby.

I stare longingly at my watch,
reminiscing a well-spent youth,
filled with a host of accolades
and brief romances.

Rain dampens my face
as darkness begins to unfold.
Suddenly, a cold blistering wind captures me
as the moon hides behind the swaying trees.

The sounds of nature grip like a vice,
a new journey tugs at my soul.
I reach for my pen.
It's just another day in the life of a writer.

STORMS OF MY CHILDHOOD

The crashing sound of thunder broke through the sky,
a streak of lightening flew across the window.
The room became eggshell white,
as my mother and I sat quietly on the bed.
One bolt came between us,
one degree of separation from death.

Frozen in our seats, we absorbed the night,
reveled in the glorious solitude,
we did not often share.
We didn't dare disturb the silence of our spirits.
We just waited patiently for the next storm.
Dad would come in on the next wave.

Sometimes it seemed the storms would last for hours.
The rage came, then violence and apathy,
as if nothing had happened.
The storms were predictable. They were always loud,
plucking our eardrums, defying our hearts in the darkness,
just before the rain.

WHEN I'M IN LOVE

When I'm in love,
time moves like a broken-winged sparrow.
The moon bursts out of the sky—
my eyes sparkle in its essence.
The earth serenades nightly appearances;
stars come together in unison
as I float along through many restless seasons.

WHAT CRUELTY LOOKS LIKE

Cruelty disturbs our well-being,
extracts life from our bones, replaces smiles with tears.
It's a cold, calculating fiend with no illumination.
Its words are blades that crudely cut into us;
our dreams spill upon the ground.

It's that nightmarish gray that seeps into us.
It's the destroyer of minds
that burns in the throats of society.
It leaves us with discontent, our feelings scattered.
We are exposed, baring our souls,
waiting for hope to appear in our silence.

SHADOW PUPPET

I am a shadow puppet,
playing in your light.
I trust you to take me along,
to seize the tender moments,
share the moon's glow.

I long to walk on my own,
not in the form of another.
I want to lounge under an oak tree,
be teased by the wind,
flirt with the sun.

I am weary of posing as your twin.
I want my own footprints in the sand,
be the pilot of my own dreams,
wake to the sound of my own heartbeat.
For once, I want the daylight on my face.

BEACHCOMBER

He drops in like a wave,
rushing the beach, scouring for treasure.
The salt-sea air licks him;
the sand tickles his bare feet.
In his pockets are pieces of the past
marred together with today's find.

An older man sits reminiscing.
He watches his grandchildren discover
the ocean's allure.
He spent countless years
chasing the life of a sailor.
Now the tide is his mirror,
reminding him why he returns year after year.

CAPTURES

I sat outside the cabin,
in the cool, summer morning,
gazing at nature's blossoms,
waiting for adventure to find me.

A bird dressed in his bird-jacket,
sat at the bottom of the door.
The sun escaped from the sky
to pose over him.

The light captured his essence
while mine disappeared
in the background
with the grayness of my soul.

In the wake of my dilemma,
Mother Nature sent a rainbow to cover me.
Witness the colors that now bleed
from the still photograph.

CONNECTIONS WITH KARATE

The karate books remain on my shelf;
I see your face in their pages.
They are a stoic reminder of you
and the friendship we once shared.

Although tattered with age, they take me back
to when I was seven, you were seventeen.
They brought us together on our porch,
our dojo in 1960's suburbs.

Little feet sailed, piercing the air, hands wrapped, breaking
boards, punching a feedbag filled with old clothes;
I stood poised like a champion.
You were my master. I was your precocious student.
You never saw me as a girl, which brought a smile to my face.

Mother hoped karate was a phase of practicing tomboys,
that would disappear behind makeup and a purse.
I was happy being the puppet for father's amusement.
I kicked so high, as if I could touch the clouds.
I saw the way you looked at me. At the time, you were so proud
of your protégée.

Now worn with life and the darkness of time,
we have become blind.
Distance has crippled our imagination, desire is for the willing.
I can no longer bask in the vainglory of my childhood,
when agile limbs of innocence used to define our relationship.

ON A FROZEN POND

The pond sparkles like an enticing jewel
In the midst of winter
It challenges our souls
We succumb
Ice slightly breaks under our feet
Leaving tiny splinters
Our chests heave against the silence
We cling to the other side of heroism
We brace ourselves
Against the imposition of a slippery slope

NATURE'S SPA

Sun-drenched skin melts
as cooling earth extinguishes.
Tepid winds spray streams, erase layers;
Your nape is caressed in softness.
Sand beads exfoliate
as currents spill their foam.
You drink the essence of the morning,
dream of thirst-filled nights.
Waves massage the beach, your soul,
wash debris from your head,
separate you from yourself.

A SILHOUETTE OF YOU

A loving vision
With your own mystique
A cast of your likeness
Dances in the sunlight
An image in the dark
Drawn on canvas
In subdued light
The way you appear
In my dreams

THE DARK SIDE

He once embraced the dark side,
hugged it like a pillow.
He understood it, welcomed it as a friend.
He made excuses,
swept them under the rug.
The dark side rode shotgun for a while.
Now it lies in his subconscious,
waiting for the light to dissipate.

EXAMINING RAIN

I don't know why the rain sounds
like a xylophone to my ears.
It plays a soft patter on my skin
that flows past a floating sun,
in a painted sky. The thumping rhythm
skips on my soul.
As I watch the clouds burst,
it's as if God is talking to me.

BARISTA

The roar of the grind, hiss of steam,
and flavored blends are hypnotic
to the ritualistic crowd,
as a friendly, apron-clad
genie performs his magic.

He's a barista,
a coffee connoisseur
with a sensitive nose
and discriminating palate,
for the perfect cup of java.

They swarm as if he were a rock star.
Starry-eyed, they sigh from whiffs
of aromatic pleasures.
They hold their cups tight,
so eager to sip,
as they sit entranced.

He circles the room. He smiles.
He watches them file out one by one,
into their metallic themes,
into their other vices,
into their fated lives,
a little more satisfied.
Sometimes they leave a tip.

WATER ON THE VINE

An ivy plant that was half-past dead,
with dried tendrils, hardened roots,
no color in its leafy veins,
was brought back among the living.

I gave the vine fresh soil and water. It gave me purpose,
fulfillment. I nurtured it until it showed promise.
It raised its withered self to the sun,
spread like a bird to be reborn.

Just like the vine, I rose to drink the freshness,
shed my hardened skin, to breathe new life.
I longed to spread my wings
and restore light in my eyes.

SHADES OF GRAY

I live in a world
Where lies become truth
Where acceptance is reality
Where the light is a vehicle
Where dark is a void
Where a rainbow has no color left
And all that exists are shades of gray.

REFLECTIONS OF SUMMER

Accents of flowers sprinkle the earth,
as bourgeoning colors perpetuate their beauty.
Soft clouds line a pale blue sky,
while cool water caresses a mountainside.

Warm breezes sashay a grassy terrain,
upstaged by smoky pits in the distance,
As vacationers seek solace
in the season's pageantry.

Temperatures rise to unbearable heights,
while dusty lanes lead me closer to home.
Walking alone multiplies the hours,
as sweat beads upon my face.

Sounds of water fascinate
as the lake comes into view.
Bathers bask in the glow of a steamy sun,
not bothered by an envious stare.

Iron-pumped torsos in skimpy apparel
swarm cabins nearby.
Just beyond the hills, an inner city awakens.
Billboards flicker, as arduous days become fun-filled nights.

LIFE AS RAIN

The rain came down like a baby's first steps,
soft, yet deliberate, cautiously scattered.

At first, I ran to avoid the droplets,
as they entered my path.

As I moved towards a destination,
I was blinded by unavoidable storms.

Now I am free to skip through the downpours,
while waiting for that elusive rainbow.

INSIDE A DESK DRAWER

Inside a desk drawer are tokens of her past
Torn treasures that cannot be replaced
She folds them like the letter that was not sent
She records another piece of herself in her diary
She holds a dusty photograph of her youth
They once had meaning in her heart
Now they are just memories
Tucked away in the dark,
Along with her tears

JOY OF WATERFALLS

Waterfalls have a way of making
the world stop and take notice.
The euphonic sounds are refreshing
gushes from a mountainside.

They're silent paradises encapsulated in nature;
clear bodies of elegance spilling over jagged rock.
As they stream upon the landscape,
we want to inhale their purity.

WINDMILLS

Against picturesque skies,
large spinning vanes
from the industrial age,
appeared as ghostly shadows
in the sunlight.

They were mysterious entities
that left shivers on our skin,
wonder in our eyes.

They became our lifelines.
They stood tall like gods;
We were below seeking answers.

Once a source of great power,
windmills like past generations,
are left oxidizing
in the winds of time.

SECRETS

Secluded affairs, kept like precious jewels
Endure for lifetimes
Clash with our soul
Remain an albatross.
Ecliptic thoughts buried deep in the recesses
Trip upon the tongue, tear at the heart,
Stray one to another, steeped in controversy.

SHY GIRL

Once hidden from the world
Of her own volition
Her silence rewarded
Her soul abandoned

Now she's learning to trust
Learning to love
Learning to speak
On her own terms

No longer self-conscious
No longer in fear
No longer lost
In need of direction

She's accepted by a few,
She's accepted by herself
To become more than
A whimper in the dark

SPARE LIGHT

I wandered about in infinite night,
my vision impaired.
It was as if society had blinded me.

I came upon a stranger.
I asked him for spare light.
He pointed to me, saying, "It comes from within."

Was I suffering temporary blindness?
Was I really living in darkness
or was my light the brightest after all?

FROM A BIRD'S EYE

Blinded by the rays,
haunted by the hills,
while we round the Magnolias.

Rippled pond
reflects broken silhouettes
of creatures above and below.

Swatting gnats with no objection,
listening with intent,
lips moisten with satisfaction.

Warm breezes brush through our hair.
We connect, disconnect time;
Our souls unlock the treasures.

THE SEA SPEAKS

The sea speaks softly like a cat's purr.
It splashes about to get my attention.
It whispers sweet nothings
to woo me.
It's as if it knows my name.

The sea quietly rolls in like a casual sun.
It caresses the shore with gentle waves,
tempts with warm, playful breezes.
I drift along,
caught in its flirtation.

BREAKING THROUGH THE SILENCE

Break through the silence with laughter
Dare to go beyond the boundaries
Of life's quiet intersection
Where you stay hidden
Waiting for permission to utter a word
Your lips strain and tremble to release your soul
The music that reflects reality
And raises consciousness
Lift your spirit out of the dead calm
Where your light is still a cautionary tale of promise
Your mind is on overdrive
Let it live out loud

MOONLIT BAY

The soft sliver of a moon hovers over the bay as it sleeps.
The moon's essence is captured by the still water;
it delivers just enough light to frame the scene
like a painting.
The city slips quietly into the background
of a foggy night.
The pier becomes an enticing figure
whisking me away under its romantic charm.
The bridge's silhouette is outlined in the distance;
it's blended against the stars towering over me,
a traveler down below, moved by
the subdued highlights of San Francisco.

ZEN STATE

The leaves are rustling
like whispered breaths
in my ears.
Emotions are held in abeyance.
I listen closely as
Mother Nature's sermon
heals my soul.

BEACON

Immortalized on canvas,
an architectural work of art,
stood against nature
to shine on the world.

Keepers of its light brought ships home
over rip-roaring tides and foggy nights.
Haunting mysteries and romantic tales
were spun in its name.

It's an ancient beauty trapped in time;
a ghost on the waterways,
that's still luminescent,
just as the tide greets the shore,
the lighthouse beckons.

Other Writing Credits-short list

The Juanita J. Martin LVN Scholarship

The Juanita J. Martin LVN scholarship was the first one for Napa Valley College. The scholarship gave $500 to a full-time or part-time vocational nursing student.
It was written and funded by Juanita J. Martin, LVN.
An LVN scholarship was awarded in the years 1999-2004.
It can be found at www.napavalley.edu

Soul Stirrings CD

The Soul Stirrings CD is an inspirational blend of original poetry and original jazz music, that was professionally mixed in a studio. Juanita J. Martin wrote all of the poetry on this CD.
It is available on www.cdbaby.com.

Acquisitions Editor- Redwood Branch- California Writers Club

As Acquisitions Editor, Juanita J. Martin wrote several articles and edited the poetry page, known as *Poetry Place* for *The Redwood Writer* newsletter.
Archived issues can be found at www.redwoodwriters.org

Other Writing-Related Credits-short list

First poet to have an open mike poetry series
in Barnes & Noble - Fairfield in 2001

Won 1st place- Sonoma County Library Slam Contest – 2005

Panelist/Author-Cotati Conversations Author Event -2008

Panelist/Author-A Celebration of Authors Event –
Solano County Library Foundation-2008

Created and hosted UniverSoul open mike series – 2008-2011

. . . as the tide greets the shore, the lighthouse beckons

NOTES

"Owners of the Light" was read at the Petaluma Poetry of Remembrance Program in 2011. (pg1)

"Bats in the Corridor" is based on actual events in 2010. (pg3)

"Invisible" was inspired by my brief employment as a bus person in 1985, prior to Air Force Basic Training. (pg6)

"Night Watch" is based on my employment as a guard in the 1990's. (pg8)

"Waiting Room" was inspired by actual events in the hospital in 2011. (pg16)

"Never said Goodbye" won 3rd place in the Solano County Fair in 2010. (pg19)

"Soul Dance" was inspired by actual events. (pg36)

"Landscape of Winter" won 3rd honorable mention, in the Ina Coolbrith Annual Poetry Contest, 2007. (pg42)

"High School Madness" was inspired by events in my high school years, 1976-1980. (pg45)

"Art Embraces the Past" is based on my interpretation of an exhibit in the Vallejo Naval History Museum in 2005. (pg51)

"Van Gogh's Summer" won the Honor Scroll Award in the 2011 Senior Poet Laureate contest. (pg56)

"Blizzard of 1983" is based on actual events that happened in Atlantic City, NJ. (pg59)

NOTES (cont'd)

"A River Runs through Me" was first published
in *Bay Area Poets Review* online edition, 2011. (pg60)

"Unbridled" was first printed in *Current Shores* Anthology
in Benicia. This is a different version of the poem. (pg67)

"Fireflies" was inspired by events in my childhood. (pg69)

"The Peace of Night" first appeared in *The Redwood Writer*,
Redwood Branch - California Writers Club. (pg70)

"Storms of my Childhood" is based on actual events in my
childhood. (pg72)

"Connections with Karate" is based on actual
karate lessons with my brother George. (pg78)

"Nature's Spa" first appeared in *The Redwood Writer,*
Redwood Branch - California Writers Club. (pg80)

"Water on the Vine" is based on actual events. (pg85)

"Reflections of Summer" was first published in
Windows & Skylights Anthology in Benicia. (pg87)

"Shy Girl" is based on my childhood. (pg93)

"From a Bird's Eye" won 3rd place
in the Solano County Fair, 2010. (pg95)